DAVID M.   .A

The Student Athletes Playbook

Hacks And Strategies For Thriving As A Student Athlete

Copyright © 2023 by David Moya

All rights reserved. No part of this publication may be reproduced, stored or transmitted in any form or by any means, electronic, mechanical, photocopying, recording, scanning, or otherwise without written permission from the publisher. It is illegal to copy this book, post it to a website, or distribute it by any other means without permission.

David Moya asserts the moral right to be identified as the author of this work.

David Moya has no responsibility for the persistence or accuracy of URLs for external or third-party Internet Websites referred to in this publication and does not guarantee that any content on such Websites is, or will remain, accurate or appropriate.

Designations used by companies to distinguish their products are often claimed as trademarks. All brand names and product names used in this book and on its cover are trade names, service marks, trademarks and registered trademarks of their respective owners. The publishers and the book are not associated with any product or vendor mentioned in this book. None of the companies referenced within the book have endorsed the book.

First edition

This book was professionally typeset on Reedsy.
Find out more at reedsy.com

Contents

1	Introduction	1
2	Time Management For Student Athletes	3
3	Academic Performance Hacks	7
4	Building A Champion's Mindset	12
5	Nutrition And Performance Optimization	16
6	Injury Prevention and Recovery	19
7	Balancing Social Life And Commitments	22
8	Conclusion	25
9	Resources	27

1

Introduction

Being a student athlete is a rewarding and challenging experience that requires balancing academic responsibilities and athletic commitments. The pursuit of excellence in both domains can often be overwhelming, leading to unique challenges that demand effective strategies and a resilient mindset. This guide acknowledges the immense commitment required to balance between academic achievement and athletic performance. It explores the nutritional, technological, and psychosocial strategies for maximizing the performance, effectiveness, and well-being of student athletes.

Unlike their peers who solely focus on academics or sports, student athletes face distinctive challenges that must be understood and mastered. On one hand, they invest significant time and energy to excel in their chosen sport. Being a student athlete demands discipline, dedication, and determination to overcome any challenges that are thrown their way. Since they not only represent themselves but also schools and communities, the pressure to perform may exert immense pressure and time constraints on their academic and athletic endeavors.

At the same time, student athletes must meet the same academic standards as their non-athlete peers and must balance a rigorous academic workload with their sporting commitments. Maintaining these high academic standards with demanding coursework alongside intense physical activities, student athletes may grapple with finding the right balance between their studies and athletic performance.

Achieving success as a student athlete centers on the ability to balance academic pursuits and athletic commitments. Research has shown that effective time management, goal setting, and maintaining a positive mindset are essential factors in achieving academic and athletic excellence. Research also suggests that academic and athletic pursuits are not mutually exclusive but rather interconnected and mutually reinforcing. Student athletes who successfully balance their priorities are more likely to experience improved academic performance, enhanced athletic outcomes, and reduced stress. Balance can unleash the full potential of student athletes, paving the way for career development, personal growth, and fulfillment.

This book provides an extensive overview of practical hacks and strategies designed to empower student athletes to excel in their academic and athletic pursuits. Throughout the following chapters, we will explore effective time management techniques, academic performance hacks, mental fortitude building, nutrition and performance optimization, injury prevention and recovery methods, and strategies for balancing social life and commitments. These evidence-based strategies aim to equip student athletes with the necessary tools to navigate the challenges they encounter and foster a holistic approach to achieving success both on and off the field/court.

2

Time Management For Student Athletes

Prioritizing Academics And Sports Effectively

Prioritizing academics and sports involves understanding the importance of each and allocating time and effort accordingly. Research indicates that effective prioritization positively influences academic performance and athletic achievements for student athletes. Student athletes should recognize that academics and sports are interdependent and complement each other in their overall development. While academic success lays the foundation for future career opportunities and personal growth, sports contribute to physical fitness, mental well-being, and valuable life skills, such as discipline and teamwork.

Student athletes should assess their academic and athletic commitments realistically and set clear goals for each to enhance prioritization. They should identify key academic deadlines and competition schedules to plan their time efficiently. By doing this, a student athlete can avoid any last-minute rushes that often result in underperformance due to not being prepared. Developing time management skills can help students plan accordingly and allocate specific time for studying and training.

Creating Efficient Study And Training Schedules

Efficient study and training schedules play a crucial role in optimizing a student athlete's performance in academics and sports. The demands of being a student athlete can be overwhelming, with classes, assignments, trainings, and competitions taking up a lot of time. Without a well-structured schedule, it becomes challenging to allocate sufficient time for academic study and to maintain sports commitments. Besides helping student athletes to manage their time effectively, study and training schedules also reduce stress and prevent anxiety, disorientation, and confusion. By establishing a structured routine, student athletes can foster a sense of control over their daily activities, leading to improved focus and productivity in both domains.

The first step in creating an efficient study and training schedule is to identify the specific academic and sports commitments for each day, week, or month. This includes class times, assignment due dates, examination schedules, training sessions, and competition schedules. Having a clear overview of obligations can help student athletes avoid conflicts and secure time for each activity. Next, student athletes should establish designated study periods within their schedule. These designated study periods need to be free from distractions so you can take full advantage of them. If the study periods become tiring, incorporating short breaks between them can promote mental rejuvenation, leading to improved retention and concentration. Student athletes should set flexible study sessions, find conducive environments to study, and set smart study goals to enhance productivity and prevent procrastination.

When designing training schedules, coaches and student athletes should work together to review, program, and organize their study and training schedules. Coaches can help with making sure you are working on the right things that will translate over to the field/court. Developing a flexible, rigorous, and objective training program can maximize the benefits of each session. Communicating academic obligations with coaches and teachers can help enable student athletes to plan training schedules that align with study periods, preventing excessive fatigue or burnout.

Finally, it is crucial to maintain consistency and flexibility within the schedule. While adhering to a structured routine is vital for time management, student athletes should also be adaptable to unforeseen circumstances, such as changes in class schedules or last-minute competition adjustments. Maintaining a flexible mindset allows student athletes to adjust their schedules accordingly without compromising their academic or athletic pursuits.

Goal Setting For Academic And Athletic Achievements

Goal setting is a crucial aspect of time management for student athletes because it provides a clear direction and purpose for their academic and athletic endeavors. Establishing specific, measurable, achievable, relevant, and time-bound (SMART) goals helps student athletes stay focused, motivated, and organized, leading to improved performance in both academics and sports. Student athletes who set specific goals are more likely to actually achieve these goals and have the motivation and perseverance to overcome difficulties along the way. Hence, setting goals aligns academic and athletic priorities, making it easier for student athletes to maintain balance and focus on their objectives.

The steps below outline how student athletes can set SMART goals for academic and athletic achievement.

- Step 1 – Identify academic and athletic aspirations to enhance clarity and focus.
- Step 2 – Set goals that are specific and measurable. For instance, instead of saying "I want to improve my grades," set a SMART goal like "I will achieve an A grade in my math course this semester."
- Step 3 – Ensure that goals are achievable and relevant based on your athletic and academic abilities, resources, and time constraints
- Step 4 – Assign timelines and deadlines to each goal
- Step 5 – Create the steps and actions required to achieve each goal
- Step 6 – Continuously track progress towards each goal and celebrate achievements, however small.

3

Academic Performance Hacks

Study Techniques For Improved Learning and Retention

Student athletes who adopt effective study techniques optimize their learning and promote long-term knowledge retention. Research shows that not all study techniques are equal – some techniques are more effective than others in facilitating learning and comprehension. Some practical study techniques that enhance academic performance include active learning, summarization and visualization, self-testing, and establishing a conducive and consistent study environment.

Active learning is a teaching and learning approach that uses participatory and interactive activities to engage students in the learning process through critical thinking, problem-solving, and collaboration. Active learning activities can include group discussions, peer teaching, roleplays, simulations, and other interactive tasks that promote deeper understanding and knowledge retention. One effective technique that can enhance learning and retention among student athletes is the use of flashcards. Flashcards help students recall information and test themselves, reinforcing their memory and enhancing recollection during exams. Group discussions and peer teaching also allow student athletes to learn from their peers' perspectives, fostering collaborative learning and providing opportunities to clarify doubts and reinforce learning.

Summarization and visualization also enhance students' learning and retention. Summarization is the art of condensing information and presenting the key ideas of a study material into concise and coherent notes. It can involve creating concept maps, flowcharts, or diagrams to visualize the relationships between different topics. Student athletes who adopt creative learning strategies, such as summarization and visualization, enhance their memory and comprehension by breaking down complex topics into self-generated notes and avoiding unnecessary and repetitive details.

Self-testing is a study technique where learners actively test themselves on the material they have learned rather than passively rereading it. It involves using quizzes, practice questions, or flashcards to recall information from memory without the aid of external cues. This technique can help student athletes to enhance their academic learning and retention by strengthening memory retrieval, identifying knowledge gaps, and improving metacognition.

Establishing a conducive and consistent study routine and environment also plays a crucial role in enhancing learning and retention. Finding a healthy study environment, like a library, can help create a positive and focused learning atmosphere that fosters academic success. Adopting a well structured and consistent study routine, combined with a healthy study environment, is a recipe that can minimize distractions, reduce procrastination, promote time management, and improve productivity.

Balancing Academic Workload With Sports Commitments

Balancing academic workload with sports commitments is a critical challenge for student athletes because they must effectively manage their time, resources, and energy. However, student athletes can implement several strategies to achieve this balance. First, they should openly communicate with their professors and coaches to create a support system that accommodates their dual responsibilities. Sharing their athletic schedules and academic commitments allows instructors and coaches to understand their workload and make necessary adjustments. Additionally, student athletes can use time management techniques, such as setting priorities, creating detailed study schedules, and breaking down larger tasks into manageable chunks. This structured approach enables them to allocate sufficient time for studying while still dedicating adequate time to sports training and competitions.

Balancing academic workload with sports commitments has notable advantages. First, effective time management and balance allow student athletes to maintain high academic standards while excelling in their co-curricular activities. Dedicating sufficient time to academics and athletics enables student athletes to pursue their dual ambitions simultaneously without compromising one for the other. This holistic approach enhances their overall development and personal growth, fostering a sense of fulfillment and accomplishment. Additionally, achieving equilibrium can reduce stress and prevent burnout, ensuring that student athletes remain physically and mentally healthy. Managing dual responsibilities can give a student athlete a lot of skills that can be transferred to aspects of life beyond academics and athletics. Hence, achieving a balance between academic and athletic commitments empowers student athletes to thrive academically and prepares them for success both on and off the field/court.

Utilizing Technology For Academic Success

Technology has revolutionized the way students approach learning. It plays a crucial role in promoting academic success by complementing and enhancing traditional teaching and learning methods. Integrating technology with learning offers numerous advantages, including access to volumes of educational resources and tools. Similarly, technology facilitates personalized and interactive learning experiences, addressing individual student needs and preferences. It provides opportunities for self-paced learning, allowing student athletes to study conveniently, which is particularly valuable given their demanding training schedules. Educational technology platforms and applications can track students' progress and performance, providing valuable feedback and insights that can inform their study strategies and improve their academic outcomes.

Student athletes can effectively use technology to enhance their academic success in various ways. For instance, students can remotely access online learning platforms and apps, such as e-books, video lectures, and interactive study materials. This accessibility allows students to study anytime and anywhere regardless of planned travels to distant places for athletic competitions. Additionally, note-taking applications, such as Evernote or Microsoft OneNote, can help student athletes keep track of their class notes, assignments, and study materials in a structured manner. Lastly, educational technology facilitates communication and collaboration among student athletes and their peers or teachers through virtual study groups, video conferencing, and messaging platforms. These digital tools enable seamless communication and foster a supportive learning environment, allowing students to exchange ideas, seek clarification, and collaborate on group projects despite physical distance.

4

Building A Champion's Mindset

Developing Mental Toughness For Sports And Academics

Developing mental toughness is a critical component of building a champion's mindset for student athletes. Mental toughness is the psychological resilience and ability to cope with stress, setbacks, and challenges effectively. It involves cultivating a strong mindset that allows student athletes to remain focused, determined, and confident in the face of adversity. As a student athlete, building this year after year is a crucial part of your growth not just for sport and the classroom, but for life. If you want to be able to respond to failure, perform under pressure, overcome obstacles, and achieve your goals, then working on your mental toughness must be essential.

One way to develop mental toughness is through deliberate practice and exposure to challenging situations. Deliberate practice involves engaging in focused, purposeful, and repetitive training with specific goals in mind. In sports, this could mean practicing specific skills, drills, or strategies repeatedly to enhance performance. Similarly, in academics, deliberate practice may involve setting aside dedicated study sessions to tackle difficult subjects or concepts. Through consistent and focused effort, student athletes gradually build resilience and develop the mental fortitude required to cope with the demands of sports and academics.

Another way to improve mental toughness is through mentorship and guidance. Having access to mentors, coaches, or academic advisors who understand the challenges of balancing sports and academics can strengthen student athletes' psychological aptitude. Research shows that mentorship positively influences the mental toughness of student athletes because it instills a sense of belonging, fosters resilience, and promotes a growth mindset. Student athletes who learn from experienced individuals obtain reliable support, valuable insights, and practical advice that enhances their mental toughness.

Managing Stress And Pressure Effectively

The ability of student athletes to attain well-being, optimize performance, and balance their academic and athletic commitments depends on their capacity to manage stress and pressure effectively. Stress and pressure are common experiences for student athletes due to the demands of rigorous training, competition, and academic responsibilities. Research indicates that chronic stress can have detrimental effects on physical and mental health, negatively impacting athletic performance and academic outcomes. Therefore, developing effective stress management techniques is crucial for student athletes to thrive in their dual roles and foster a champion's mindset.

An effective stress management strategy for student athletes is cognitive reframing or cognitive reappraisal. Cognitive reframing involves identifying negative thoughts or stress-inducing situations and reinterpreting them in a more positive or constructive light. Student athletes can apply cognitive reframing techniques to stressful situations related to sports, academics, or their overall life. For example, when facing a challenging competition or exam, they can reframe their thoughts from "I am not prepared for this" to "I have trained hard and studied diligently, and I am capable of handling this challenge." By reframing negative thoughts and embracing a positive perspective, student athletes can reduce anxiety, boost self-confidence, and approach stressors with a more composed and resilient mindset.

In addition to cognitive reframing, practicing relaxation techniques can effectively reduce stress and pressure for student athletes. Techniques such as deep breathing, progressive muscle relaxation, and mindfulness-based stress reduction have been shown to have a positive impact on reducing stress and promoting overall well-being. Engaging in regular relaxation practices can help student athletes manage their physiological and psychological responses to stress, promoting a sense of calmness and clarity. These characteristics are essential when it is time to perform in a high pressure game or a final exam in the classroom.

Visualization And Affirmations For Peak Performance

Visualization and affirmations are powerful mental tools that can enhance peak performance for student athletes in academics and athletics. Research has shown that the mind-body connection plays a significant role in optimizing performance. Visualization involves creating vivid mental pictures of successful performances or outcomes to experience improved self-confidence and reduced performance anxiety. When student athletes visualize themselves performing well in a competition or an exam, they are more likely to translate their mental images into actual actions. Studies have shown that athletes who regularly use visualization techniques report higher levels of self-efficacy and focus, which positively impact their performance outcomes.

Affirmations are positive statements repeated to oneself to reinforce beliefs and attitudes that support peak performance. These statements are typically written in the present tense and reflect specific goals or attributes that the student athlete aims to exemplify. For example, an affirmation may be "I am strong, capable, and fully prepared to excel in my academics and sports." By repeating affirmations consistently, you can create a positive and empowering internal dialogue that counteracts self-doubt and negative thinking. Numerous studies have demonstrated the effectiveness of affirmations in enhancing self-confidence, motivation, and overall performance. When student athletes believe in their abilities and affirm their potential for success, they are more likely to approach challenges with a growth mindset and persevere in the face of obstacles.

Harnessing the full potential of visualization and affirmations requires consistency, regularity, and intentionality. Student athletes should visualize in quiet and focused moments, such as before bedtime or during relaxation exercises, by paying attention to sensory details such as sights, sounds, and feelings associated with success. Since visualizations and affirmations are most effective when integrated with disciplined and purposeful practice, student athletes should work hard in their academic and athletic pursuits, using these tools as much as they can to enhance their overall performance.

5

Nutrition And Performance Optimization

Understanding The Role Of Nutrition In Sports And Academics

Proper nutrition provides the body with the necessary nutrients, energy, and building blocks to support athletic performance and academic endeavors. The foods and beverages that student athletes consume directly impact their energy levels, cognitive function, recovery, and overall well-being. In sports, nutrition plays a significant role in an athlete's ability to train, compete, and recover effectively. Adequate nutrition supports the energy demands of physical activities, such as strength training, endurance exercises, and skill development. In academics, nutrition supports cognitive function, memory, concentration, and overall mental well-being. The brain relies on a steady supply of nutrients to function optimally, and certain foods have been linked to improved cognitive performance and academic achievement. Understanding the relationship between nutrition, sports, and academics is vital for student athletes to achieve overall success. The physical and mental demands of being a student and an athlete need the proper nutrition to address those demands. Having a balanced diet containing macronutrients (carbohydrates, proteins, and fats) and micronutrients (vitamins and minerals) maintains energy levels, supports immune function, and promotes overall well-being.

Creating A Personalized Diet Plan For Student Athletes

Personalized diet plans help student athletes meet their unique nutritional needs and optimize their athletic performance and academic achievements. A personalized diet plan takes into account the individual athlete's energy expenditure, macronutrient needs, micronutrient requirements, and any specific dietary restrictions or preferences, providing them with the best possible nutrition to excel in their endeavors. The first step in creating a personalized diet plan for student athletes is to assess their individual energy needs. Energy requirements can vary significantly depending on the type of sport, training intensity, and the individual's body composition. Athletes engaged in high-intensity and endurance sports may require higher caloric intake, while those in sports that prioritize strength and power may have different energy demands. Sports nutrition experts can help student athletes determine their specific energy needs and develop an appropriate caloric intake plan.

The next step is addressing macronutrient and micronutrient needs. Carbohydrates, proteins, and fats are the three primary macronutrients that provide the body with energy and essential building blocks for muscle repair and growth. On the other hand, vitamins, minerals, and antioxidants are micronutrients that facilitate physiological processes, immune function, and recovery. A personalized diet plan considers the individual's sport-specific needs and adjusts the macronutrient and micronutrient ratios accordingly. Student athletes with specific dietary preferences or restrictions, such as vegetarians, vegans, or those with food allergies, must ensure they meet their nutritional requirements according to their specifications. Personalized nutrition will enhance student athletes' sports performance, cognitive function, and overall health, fostering a balanced and successful approach to their academic and athletic commitments.

Hydration Strategies For Optimal Performance

Hydration is a critical aspect of nutrition for student athletes. Proper fluid intake supports optimal performance in sports and academics. Conversely, dehydration can have detrimental effects on athletic performance, cognitive function, and overall health, making it essential for student athletes to implement effective hydration strategies. As a student athlete, drinking water or electrolytes throughout the day has to be a high priority. You can prioritize hydration throughout the day by taking adequate fluid to maintain body temperature, support cardiovascular function, and facilitate nutrient transport to the body. Although water is the most accessible and effective source of hydration, electrolyte-containing beverages, such as sports drinks, can be beneficial for prolonged and intense exercise lasting more than one hour. Keeping a water bottle on you at all times is a sure way to remind yourself to drink water consistently throughout the day. If that doesn't help, setting hydration reminders on your phone can be very useful. Lastly, eating fruit and vegetables can also help meet hydration needs.

6

Injury Prevention and Recovery

Identifying And Preventing Common Sports Injuries

Participating in sports comes with inherent risks of injury. Student athletes must proactively identify and prevent common sports-related injuries. Identifying common sports injuries is the first step toward effective injury prevention. Student athletes, coaches, and athletic trainers should be knowledgeable about the signs and symptoms of various injuries to promptly address them. Overtraining and insufficient rest periods are prevalent among student athletes and can increase the risk of overuse injuries, such as stress fractures and tendinitis. These injuries often manifest as localized pain, swelling, and limited range of motion. Acute injuries, such as sprains, strains, and contusions, result from sudden trauma and are characterized by immediate pain, bruising, and loss of function. Preventing common sports injuries involves a comprehensive approach that encompasses proper training techniques, warm-up routines, and injury prevention programs. Coaches should emphasize the importance of proper form, biomechanics, and body mechanics to prevent stress on joints and muscles. Implementing these injury prevention strategies as part of regular training routines can significantly contribute to a safer and more productive athletic experience for student athletes.

Recovery Techniques For Student Athletes

Some of the fundamental recovery techniques for student athletes are adequate rest and sleep, proper nutrition, and active recovery techniques. Sleep plays a vital role in physical and cognitive recovery, allowing the body to repair tissues, restore energy, and consolidate learning and memory. Student athletes should prioritize consistent and sufficient sleep duration to ensure they are well-rested and prepared for their academic and athletic commitments. Proper nutrition also supports muscle repair and glycogen replenishment after intense workouts and competitions. Lastly, active recovery techniques, such as low-intensity exercises and foam rolling, are beneficial for student athletes. Engaging in light exercises, like walking or cycling, can help improve blood circulation, reduce muscle soreness, and facilitate recovery. Incorporating adequate rest, a balanced diet, and active recovery into student athlete routines supports physical activity and enhances recovery from intense training or competition demands.

Working With Sports Medicine Professionals

Sports medicine professionals, including sports physicians, athletic trainers, and physical therapists, play a crucial role in identifying, preventing, and managing sports-related injuries. They are well-trained in assessing and diagnosing sports-related injuries, enabling early identification of injuries, prompt treatment, and a minimal risk of exacerbation. Research has shown that early intervention by sports medicine professionals can significantly reduce the time student athletes spend away from their sports due to injuries. By promptly addressing injuries and implementing appropriate treatment plans, student athletes can resume their training and competitions more quickly, ensuring that their academic and athletic commitments remain on track.

In addition to injury prevention and treatment, sports medicine professionals also offer valuable guidance on proper training techniques and recovery strategies. As a student athlete, the training room should be a heavily visited place regardless of if you are injured or not. Injury prevention is just as important to focus on and sports medicine professionals can assist immensely with that. Working with sports medicine professionals offers numerous benefits for student athletes in their academic and athletic journey because these experts play a pivotal role in identifying and treating sports-related injuries, reducing the time away from sports due to injuries, and facilitating faster recovery.

7

Balancing Social Life And Commitments

The Significance Of Maintaining A Healthy Social Life For Student Athletes

Maintaining a healthy social life plays a crucial role in promoting well-being and enhancing the academic-athletic balance. Positive social interactions foster a sense of belonging, support, and companionship, promoting mental and emotional health. Student athletes that can have a well balanced social life can help reduce levels of stress and anxiety. A healthy social life provides a support system that can help student athletes navigate the challenges of balancing rigorous academic demands and intensive training schedules. Social connections offer valuable opportunities for relaxation, recreation, and stress relief, which are vital for preventing burnout and optimizing athletic performance. By maintaining a healthy social life, student athletes can build resilience, enhance their mental and emotional well-being, and thrive academically and athletically.

Strategies For Managing Time With Friends And Family

Effective strategies for managing your time while maintaining connections with friends and family consist of choosing quality over quantity, setting boundaries, and using technology to stay in communication with friends and loved ones who might be elsewhere. Student athletes can also integrate social activities with academic or athletic commitments by planning social events in advance to minimize conflicts and maintain a balanced schedule. Maintaining a healthy social life for student athletes brings numerous benefits, such as reducing stress and enhancing overall well-being. These social interactions can provide emotional support, improve motivation, and foster a sense of belonging. Spending time with loved ones helps prevent feelings of isolation or burnout, ensuring that student athletes can face academic and athletic challenges with a stronger support system. Prioritizing time with friends and family will help you thrive both on and off the field/court.

Communication Skills And Overcoming Peer Pressures And Distractions

Developing effective communication skills helps student athletes maintain a balance between their relationships and responsibilities. Student athletes need to express their needs, goals, and time constraints openly with friends, family, coaches, and instructors so that everyone is on the same page and can know how to help. Effective communication skills enable student athletes to manage their social life, navigate their academic and athletic responsibilities, and experience reduced stress.

Peer pressure can be one of the biggest distractions that can lead you astray if you continuously give in to it. You're going to have friends that don't have the same priorities or responsibilities that you do. That is just the way it is. There will be times that these friends might want to go out on a weeknight, (when you may have classes the next day) and try to convince you to go with them. It's your job to have the discipline to see the bigger picture and prioritize going to class the next morning or being ready for an early morning practice. That might mean you have to decide to sit that one out that night. They might be mad at you, but it will only be temporary. If they can't get past it, then maybe you need to find some new friends. It is very important to develop a strong sense of self-awareness and have the ability to resist these peer pressure temptations. Implementing time management strategies and creating a consistent study environment can help you reduce distractions and maintain focus. If you can make these adjustments and create these consistent habits, you should have a great recipe for success in all facets of a student athlete's life.

8

Conclusion

This book has provided a comprehensive guide for student athletes seeking to excel in their academic pursuits and athletic endeavors. The essential hacks and evidence-based strategies discussed are designed to equip student athletes with time management techniques, academic performance optimization, mental fortitude, nutritional knowledge, injury management skills, and strategies for maintaining a healthy social life. These strategies are designed to help student athletes overcome the unique challenges they face every day and foster a balanced and resilient mindset.

Student athletes should internalize and implement the nutritional, technological, and psychosocial techniques shared in this book to unlock their full potential both on and off the field/court. In summary, they should create structured study and training schedules, set SMART goals, eat balanced diets and maintain proper hydration, collaborate with their coaches and teachers through mentorship, leverage technology for academic success, develop mental toughness through intentional and consistent practice, use visualization and affirmations for peak performance, work closely with sports medicine experts, and maintain healthy relationships to balance their academic and athletic responsibilities.

Integrating these strategies into their daily lives will help student athletes build a robust and resilient mindset that gives them the confidence and determination to balance their academics and athletics. The nuggets shared in this book offer a holistic approach to cultivating a champion's mindset, improving mental and physical well-being, and achieving personal growth and fulfillment. With discipline, dedication, and determination, student athletes can successfully overcome barriers to their dual responsibilities and become well-rounded individuals who excel academically, athletically, and beyond.

9

Resources

Abdurakhmonova, Z. Y. (2022). The Role of Modern Pedagogical Technologies in Improving the Quality of the Educational Process. Экономика и социум, (3-2 (94)), 12-16.

Aryanto, D. B., & Larasati, A. (2020, January). Factors influencing mental toughness. In 5th ASEAN Conference on Psychology, Counselling, and Humanities (ACPCH 2019) (pp. 307-309). Atlantis Press.

Bird, M. D., Simons, E. E., & Jackman, P. C. (2021). Mental toughness, sport-related well-being, and mental health stigma among National Collegiate Athletic Association Division I student-athletes. Journal of Clinical Sport Psychology, 15(4), 306-322.

Condello, G., Capranica, L., Doupona, M., Varga, K., & Burk, V. (2019). Dual-career through the elite university student-athletes' lenses: The international FISU-EAS survey. PloS one, 14(10), e0223278. Garcia, M. G., & Subia, G. (2019). High school athletes: Their motivation, study habits, self-discipline and academic performance. International Journal of Physical Education, Sports and Health, 6(1), 86-90.

Davies, M. A., Lawrence, T., Edwards, A., Lecky, F., McKay, C. D., Stokes, K. A., & Williams, S. (2020). Serious sports-related injury in England and Wales from 2012-2017: a study protocol. Injury epidemiology, 7, 1-10.

Dunford, M., & Doyle, J. A. (2021). Nutrition for sport and exercise. Cengage Learning.

Forte-Celaya, J., Ibarra, L., & Glasserman-Morales, L. D. (2021). Analysis of creative thinking skills development under active learning strategies. Education Sciences, 11(10), 621.

Guest, N. S., Horne, J., Vanderhout, S. M., & El-Sohemy, A. (2019). Sport nutrigenomics: personalized nutrition for athletic performance. Frontiers in nutrition, 6, 8.

Haleem, A., Javaid, M., Qadri, M. A., & Suman, R. (2022). Understanding the role of digital technologies in education: A review. Sustainable Operations and Computers, 3, 275-285.

Hodges, B. C. (2022). Collaborative initiative to improve DIII student-athlete well-being. Journal of Athlete Development and Experience, 4(1), 2.

Liew, G. C., Kuan, G., Chin, N. S., & Hashim, H. A. (2019). Mental toughness in sport. German Journal of Exercise and Sport Research, 49(4), 381-394.

Linnér, L., Stambulova, N., & Ziegert, K. (2021). Maintaining dual career balance: a scenario perspective on Swedish university student-athletes' experiences and coping. Scandinavian Journal of Sport and

Exercise Psychology, 3, 47-55.

Lopes Dos Santos, M., Uftring, M., Stahl, C. A., Lockie, R. G., Alvar, B., Mann, J. B., & Dawes, J. J. (2020). Stress in academic and athletic performance in collegiate athletes: A narrative review of sources and monitoring strategies. Frontiers in sports and active living, 2, 42.

Miller, A. (2022). "The Centerpiece of College Athletics": Prioritizing Education in the College Sports Reform Movement. Journal of Intercollegiate Sport, 15(1), 28-51.

Motevalli, S., Sulaiman, T., Wong, K. Y., & Jaafar, W. M. W. (2022). Athletes' Psycho-physical Training and Cognitive Restructuring Module To Enhance University-athlete Students' Well-being. The Open Psychology Journal, 15(1).

Muljana, P. S., & Luo, T. (2019). Factors contributing to student retention in online learning and recommended strategies for improvement: A systematic literature review. Journal of Information Technology Education: Research, 18.

Nafilla, D., Dewi, Y. L. R., & Ellyas, I. S. (2023, July). The Relationship between Nutritional Knowledge and Nutritional Status in Sports Special Class Students. In The Third International Conference on Innovations in Social Sciences Education and Engineering (Vol. 1, No. 1, pp. 005-005).

Putukian, M. (2018). The psychological response to injury in student athletes: a narrative review with a focus on mental health. British Journal of Sports Medicine, 50(3), 145-148.

Ramdani, A., Syukur, A., Gunawan, G., Permatasari, I., & Yustiqvar, M. (2020). Increasing Students' Metacognition Awareness: Learning Studies Using Science Teaching Materials Based on SETS Integrated Inquiry. International Journal of Advanced Science and Technology, 29(5), 6708-6721.

Riviere, A. J., Leach, R., Mann, H., Robinson, S., Burnett, D. O., Babu, J. R., & Frugé, A. D. (2021). Nutrition knowledge of collegiate athletes in the United States and the impact of sports dietitians on related outcomes: A narrative review. Nutrients, 13(6), 1772.

Şahin, E., Çekin, R., & Yazıcılar Özçelik, İ. (2018). Predictors of academic achievement among physical education and sports undergraduate students. Sports, 6(1), 8.

Sadigursky, D., Braid, J. A., De Lira, D. N. L., Machado, B. A. B., Carneiro, R. J. F., & Colavolpe, P. O. (2018). The FIFA 11+ injury prevention program for soccer players: a systematic review. BMC sports science, medicine, and rehabilitation, 9(1), 1-8.

Sainsbury, D. A., Downs, J., Netto, K., & McKenna, L. J. (2023). Factors Associated with Sports Injuries in Adolescents Who Play Team Sports at a Non-elite Level: A Scoping Review. JOSPT Open, (0), 1-34.

Sullivan, M., Moore, M., Blom, L. C., & Slater, G. (2020). Relationship between social support and depressive symptoms in collegiate student athletes. Journal for the Study of Sports and Athletes in Education, 14(3), 192-209.

The Self-Testing Toolkit. (2023). Ivybridge Community College. https://www.ivybridge.devon.sch.uk/sttk

RESOURCES

Yalcin, Y., & Turan, F. (2021). Are Self-Talk and Mental Toughness Level Prerequisites besides the Kick Boxing Education Level in Athletes?. International Education Studies, 14(10), 105-115.

Zung, I., Imundo, M. N., & Pan, S. C. (2022). How do college students use digital flashcards during self-regulated learning?. Memory, 30(8), 923-941.

Printed in Great Britain
by Amazon